STAND UP: Bullying Prevention

What to Do if YOU Are BULLIED

Addy Ferguson

PowerKiDS press

New York

Published in 2013 by The Rosen Publishing Group, Inc.
29 East 21st Street, New York, NY 10010

First Edition

Editor: Jennifer Way
Book Design: Erica Clendening and Colleen Bialecki

Photo Credits: Cover © iStockphoto.com/Craig Dingle; p. 5 Leanne Temme/Photo Library/Getty Images; p. 6 Henry King/Taxi/Getty Images; p. 7 Sandy Jones/Photodisc/Getty Images; p. 8 © iStockphoto.com/ Omgimages; p. 9 David Harry Stewart/Stone/Getty Images; p. 11 © iStockphoto.com/Imagesbybarbara; p. 12 SW Productions/Stockbyte/Getty Images; p. 13 Rob Lewine/Getty Images; p. 14 Adrian Samson/Stone/ Getty Images; p. 15 Echo/Cultura/Getty Images; p. 16 Robert Warren/Taxi/Getty Images; p. 17 Digital Vision/ Getty Images; p. 18 Peter Dazely/Photographer's Choice/Getty Images; p. 19 © iStockphoto.com/Christopher Futcher; p. 20 Yellow Dog Productions/The Image Bank/Getty Images; p. 21 Jeff Dunn/Photo Library/Getty Images; p. 22 KidStock/Blend Images/Getty Images.

Library of Congress Cataloging-in-Publication Data

Ferguson, Addy.
 What to do if you are bullied / by Addy Ferguson. — 1st ed.
     p. cm. — (Stand up: bullying prevention)
 Includes index.
 ISBN 978-1-4488-9665-3 (library binding) — ISBN 978-1-4488-9788-9 (pbk.) —
 ISBN 978-1-4488-9789-6 (6-pack)
 1. Bullying. 2. Bullying—Prevention. 3. Self-esteem. I. Title.
 BF637.B85F47 2013
 302.34'3—dc23

                                   2012018696

Manufactured in the United States of America

CPSIA Compliance Information: Batch #W13PK4: For Further Information contact Rosen Publishing, New York, New York at 1-800-237-9932

Contents

What Is Bullying? 4

Types of Bullying 6

Why Do People Bully? 8

The Effects of Bullying 10

Walk Away 12

Fighting Is Wrong 14

Talk to an Adult 16

Self-Esteem 18

A Bully-Free Zone....................................... 20

No One Deserves to Be Bullied...................... 22

Glossary 23

Index.. 24

Websites 24

What Is Bullying?

Have you or a friend ever been picked on or teased over and over again by classmates in the lunchroom or playground? Have you been bumped or pushed in the halls or made to feel bad on the bus? When someone **taunts** or hurts another person over and over again, he or she is a bully.

Bullying other people is wrong. It happens all the time, though. This does not mean it is OK or that it cannot be stopped. Each of us has the power to stand up and stop bullying. Are you ready to find out how?

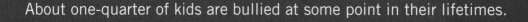

About one-quarter of kids are bullied at some point in their lifetimes.

5

Types of Bullying

Did you know there is more than one kind of bullying? Some bullying is **physical**. This kind of bullying takes the form of pushing, hitting, or hurting a person's body or her belongings in some way.

Even though physical bullying is the easiest to see, it is the least common form of bullying. Only about one-third of all bullying is physical.

Cyberbullies may send very cruel text messages because they would not say those words face-to-face.

Verbal bullying is calling people names, teasing them, or telling lies about them. Cyberbullying is a special kind of bullying that happens over the Internet, through text messages, or through e-mail. Bullies can also hurt their **victims** by ignoring or **excluding** them.

Why Do People Bully?

There are many reasons why people bully. Some bullies treat others badly because they do not feel good about themselves. Other bullies have parents who are bullies. Often, bullies may not feel connected to others and do not have feelings of **empathy** toward other people. On the other hand, they may have plenty of friends and feel that bullying makes them more **popular**.

Kids who are loners or who are seen as "different" from their peers in some way are more likely to be bullied.

Bullies may be troublemakers at home, or they may come from homes where there is a lot of fighting.

No matter what the reasons are, bullying is wrong. Researchers, parents, and teachers across the country have been working to educate people about bullying. If enough people know what to look for and what to do, bullying can be stopped.

The Effects of Bullying

Bullying can have real and lasting effects. If you have been bullied, you may feel hopeless, scared, humiliated, angry, or like no one cares. All of these feelings are normal.

People who have been bullied may not want to go to school. Their grades are likely to drop, too. Bullying can cause low **self-esteem**, **depression**, and **anxiety**. If it is allowed to go on for a long time, some victims go to great lengths to stop the pain, including killing themselves or others. Even without these extreme effects, none of the effects of bullying are good ones.

A person who is being bullied may feel overwhelmed. It is OK to have these feelings, but it is important to know that there are people who can help.

Walk Away

If you are being bullied, you might feel like there is nothing you can do to make the bullying stop. There are a few things you can try, though.

It can be hard to walk away when someone is taunting you, but it can be an effective way to deal with bullies.

Projecting confidence as you walk away denies the bully the reaction she wants. It also reminds you that you are in control of how you respond to situations.

Most bullies are looking for a reaction. They want to make their victims upset, scare them, or make them cry. Try to look your bully in the eyes, be **assertive**, and say that she should leave you alone. Then walk away. The bully did not get a reaction, so she may leave you alone in the future. If the bully tries again, tell an adult.

Fighting Is Wrong

If you are dealing with a physical bully, it may seem like the best **defense** is to fight back. Just as bullying is wrong, fighting is wrong, too. Even if the bully started the fight with you, you could get punished. You are also likely to get hurt. You could hurt the other person as well. Hurting another person is never the answer.

You might feel like fighting because you are angry about being bullied. It is OK to be angry, but that does not make it OK to fight.

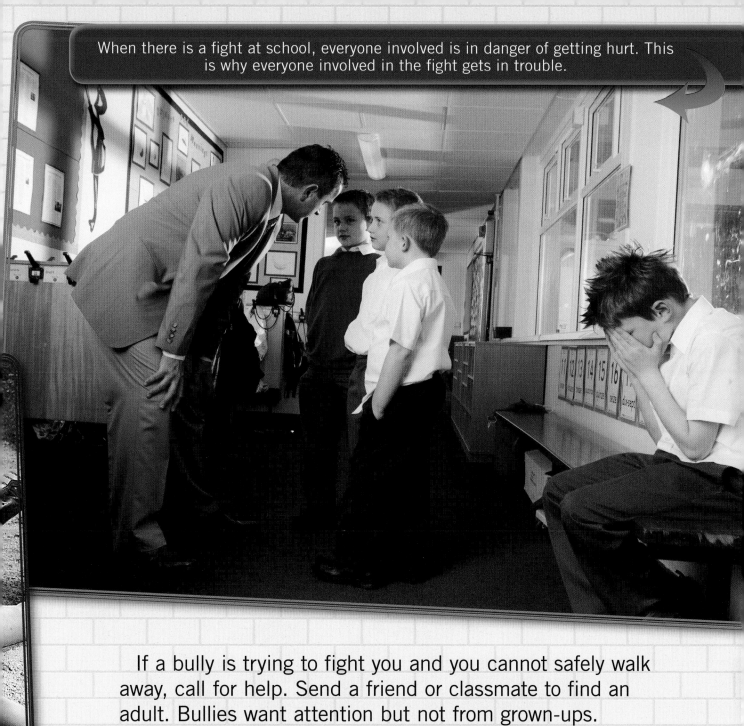

When there is a fight at school, everyone involved is in danger of getting hurt. This is why everyone involved in the fight gets in trouble.

If a bully is trying to fight you and you cannot safely walk away, call for help. Send a friend or classmate to find an adult. Bullies want attention but not from grown-ups.

Talk to an Adult

Often the victims of bullies never tell an adult. They may be afraid telling will make matters worse. They may feel that adults around them do not care and will not help them.

Only about one-third of bullied kids tell an adult about their problem.

Teachers and principals must work together with students to create a school where everyone knows that bullying will not be tolerated.

Talking to a trusted adult, such as a parent or teacher, is important, though. These people can help you talk about how you feel. They can help you make a plan to stop what is happening. Even more important, they can make a plan to make school a safer place for everyone. It truly takes a community to stop bullying.

Self-Esteem

Bullying makes people feel sad, lonely, and scared. Over time, bullying can lead to feelings of low self-esteem. These feelings can continue even after the bullying stops.

Talking to a guidance counselor can help you deal with feelings about being bullied.

Taking part in activities that make you feel good can help rebuild your self-esteem.

If you have been bullied, there are people who can help you. Talking to a trusted adult such as a school **guidance counselor** can help. She may know of groups where victims of bullies can share stories. Knowing you are not the only one who feels the way you do can help you feel better. Taking part in activities that make you feel good is another way you can rebuild your self-esteem and confidence.

A Bully-Free Zone

It takes the whole school community working together to stop bullying. It is important to talk about the rights every student should expect at school. Some of these rights include feeling safe, respecting others, and not hurting others.

It has been found that kicking bullies out of school does not solve the problem. Bullies need people to show them how to be a good friend who has empathy for others.

Playgrounds are one of the places at school where a lot of bullying happens. It is important for teachers to be present in these places to reduce bullying.

A school might decide to become a bully-free zone. That means that students must agree to stand up for bullying victims. They must do this even if the victim is not their friend, is different from them, or standing up might upset their own group of friends. This takes bravery, but it feels good to know you are doing the right thing!

No One Deserves to Be Bullied

It is important to remember that being bullied is not your fault. You did not cause it. No one deserves to be bullied.

If you have been bullied, it might help you feel better to take action. Talk to your principal about starting a "no-bullying" program at your school. Most important, if you see bullying happen to someone around you, stand up. If everyone did that, we might stop bullying in its tracks.

Everyone deserves to feel safe at school. If you are bullied, you are not alone. Now you know how to help yourself and reduce bullying at your school.

Glossary

anxiety (ang-ZY-eh-tee) Uneasiness or worry.

assertive (uh-SER-tiv) Being firm in a positive way.

defense (dih-FENTS) Something people do that helps keep them safe.

depression (dih-PREH-shun) A sickness in which a person is very sad for a long time.

empathy (EM-puh-thee) Understanding and being aware of the feelings and thoughts of another person.

excluding (eks-KLOOD-ing) Keeping or shutting someone out.

guidance counselor (GY-dins KOWN-suh-ler) Someone who helps students solve personal problems or problems with other people.

physical (FIH-zih-kul) Having to do with the body.

popular (PAH-pyuh-lur) Liked by lots of people.

self-esteem (self-uh-STEEM) Happiness with oneself.

taunts (TONTS) Makes fun of someone else or hurts his or her feelings.

verbal (VER-bul) Using words.

victims (VIK-timz) People or animals that are harmed or killed.

Index

B
body, 6
bus, 4

C
cyberbullying, 7

D
defense, 14
depression, 10

E
e-mail, 7

H
halls, 4

I
Internet, 7

K
kind, 6–7

L
lies, 7
lunchroom, 4

N
names, 7

P
playground, 4
power, 4

R
reasons, 8–9

S
self-esteem, 10,
    18–19

Websites

Due to the changing nature of Internet links, PowerKids Press has developed an online list of websites related to the subject of this book. This site is updated regularly. Please use this link to access the list: www.powerkidslinks.com/subp/wdyab/